THE LAST LAUGH

BRIAN J. BURTON

REVISED EDITION

HANBURY PLAYS

KEEPER'S LODGE
BROUGHTON GREEN
DROITWICH
WORCESTERSHIRE WR9 7EE

BY THE SAME AUTHOR

ROSMERSHOLM (a new English version)
SWEENEY TODD THE BARBER
THE MURDER OF MARIA MARTEN or THE RED BARN
LADY AUDLEY'S SECRET or DEATH IN LIME TREE WALK
THE DRUNKARD or DOWN WITH DEMON DRINK!
THREE HISSES FOR VILLAINY!!!
EAST LYNNE or NEVER CALLED ME MOTHER!
CHEERS, TEARS AND SCREAMERS!
A BEAR WITH A SORE HEAD (adapted from Chekhov)
BEING OF SOUND MIND
MURDER PLAY
DRINK TO ME ONLY
FROM THREE TO FOUR
HE AND SHE
DEATH MASQUE
THE FINAL MOVEMENT
FACE THE QUEEN
A QUESTION OF PROFIT
TEA WITH JASON
GHOST OF A CHANCE
SUDDEN DEATH
FOILED AGAIN
VISITING TIME
NINE WOMEN - NO MEN
LINES OF COMMUNICATION
THE WOODPILE
A TALE OF TWO CITIES (Adapted from Charles Dickens)

First published 1982

This revised edition first published 1990

© Brian J. Burton 1982, 1990

ISBN: 185205 090 X

CHARACTERS

THEODORE MASON - a late middle-aged Music Hall artist
ARCHIE BRIGGS - A Theatre Manager
QUEENIE TOMINO - a Music Hall artist
DORIS MALONE - an Assistant Stage Manager

THE ACTION OF THE PLAY TAKES PLACE ON THE STAGE OF A
PROVINCIAL MUSIC HALL EARLY IN THE 1950's, FOLLOWED BY
A FLASHBACK TO THE DRESSING ROOM OF THEODORE MASON
ABOUT THIRTY MINUTES EARLIER.

THE FIRST SCENE IS PLAYED IN FRONT OF A TRAVERSE CURTAIN
PAINTED IN SOME GARISH DESIGN. (OR, IF THAT IS NOT POSSIBLE,
IN FRONT OF THE STAGE CURTAINS)

THEODORE'S INTRO MUSIC IS PLAYED LOUDLY. ('HAPPY DAYS
ARE HERE AGAIN' OR 'HERE WE ARE AGAIN' OR SIMILAR) THEO
ENTERS RIGHT. HE IS DRESSED IN AN OUTRAGEOUS DRESS AND
A FLAMBOYANT WIG. HE IS HEAVILY MADE-UP IN THE STYLE OF
A PANTOMIME DAME.

THEO Well, here I am again, boys. Here I am again. Oh, but I'm
not at all happy - not at all. In fact, I'm cut to the quick
-cut to the quick I am. And I cut very quickly. Last week
I sent my photograph to the Lonely Hearts Club. I did ...
I did. And do you know what? They sent it back again -
they did - they sent it back. They said they were sorry but
they hadn't got anybody that lonely. What a life, what a
life! But I had a boy friend once though - oh what a man
he was - what a man! The trouble was that he was one
of those football fanatics. One Friday night after he'd taken
me to the pictures - back row of course. Girls, have you
ever been in the back row on a Friday night? Oh, the things
that go on there - and the things that come off as well.
Anyway, after the pictures, I said to him, 'Why don't you
come round to my place tomorrow afternoon, eh?' I thought
he might fancy some tea and crumpet. Well, they do, don't
they? Terrible appetites some of them - terrible. Anyway,
do you know what he said? You'd never guess. 'I've got a
ticket for the Cup Final tomorrow,' That's what he said.
'Oh, really,' I said, 'oh, really. What can you get from the
Cup Final that you can't get from me?' Do you know what
he said? 'Forty five minutes each way and a brass band
in between.' .... Oh, a terrible thing happened to me on
the way to the theatre tonight - terrible. I was coming
along Lovers Lane minding my own business when, all of
a sudden, this great big man jumped out at me. Ever so
big he was - all muscles and things, you know. 'First of
all I'm going to take all your money,' he said, 'and then
I'm going to have my way with you' I went all of a tremble
all over. 'Oh, dear,' I said, 'oh, dear. I haven't got a penny
on me - not a penny. Would you accept a cheque?' ... What
do you think of my figure, boys? (TURNING ROUND) I'm
trying to diet. I'm dying to try it as well - but that's another
story. Oh, I must tell you about another boy friend I had
once. Oh, yes I did. I've been a little devil in my time,
I can tell you. Anyway, this boy friend - he was a baker.

Only a little man he was ...

HE BREAKS OFF SUDDENLY AS HE IS DISTRACTED BY A NOISE IN THE WINGS.

THEO (CALLING AND RUSHING INTO THE WINGS) No, don't do that! George! Archie! Where is everybody?

THE SOUND OF A SHOT FROM THE WINGS. THIS IS FOLLOWED BY A FEW SECONDS OF SILENCE AND THEN EXCITED VOICES FROM THE WINGS. THEN, ARCHIE BRIGGS ENTERS.

ARCHIE Ladies and gentlemen - please, please! There is no cause for alarm. There has been a slight accident but the show will continue in a few minutes time. In the meantime ... one moment, please. (GOES TO THE SIDE OF THE STAGE AND HOLDS A WHISPERED CONVERSATION) I see. I see. (ADDRESSING THE AUDIENCE AGAIN) Ladies and gentlemen, I have to ask you to remain in your seats. On no account will anyone be allowed to leave the theatre. If there is a member of the medical profession in the audience, would you be so good as to come up onto the stage at once. Thank you, ladies and gentlemen - thank you.

THEO'S INTRO MUSIC IS PLAYED LOUDLY. SNAP BLACKOUT.

THE CURTAINS COME BACK ALMOST AT ONCE TO REVEAL THEODORE MASON'S DRESSING ROOM. IT IS A DRAB ROOM. THE DRESSING TABLE HAS A MIRROR SET ABOVE IT WITH A NUMBER OF LOW-POWER BULBS AROUND IT. IT IS SET AT AN ANGLE TO THE AUDIENCE SO THAT THEODORE IS FACING HALF FRONT. THERE IS A DOOR CENTRE BACK. AN ARMCHAIR PILED WITH CLOTHES, IS SET LEFT CENTRE WITH A THEATRICAL BASKET, WHICH IS ALSO PILED HIGH WITH CLOTHES, ON ITS LEFT. THEODORE IS SEATED AT THE DRESSING TABLE MAKING-UP FOR HIS ACT. (DURING THE THEATRE MANAGER'S SPEECH, THE ACTOR PLAYING THEODORE HAS REMOVED THE DRESS UNDER WHICH HE WAS WEARING THE CLOTHES HE HAS ON NOW - A SWEATSHIRT AND JEANS. HE HAS REMOVED THE WIG AND AS MUCH MAKE-UP AS IS POSSIBLE IN THE TIME) THE TANNOY BY THE DOOR IS SWITCHED OFF.

IT IS THIRTY MINUTES BEFORE THE PREVIOUS SCENE.

THERE IS A KNOCK AT THE DOOR

THEO (WITHOUT TURNING) Who is it? What do you want?
ARCHIE (OPENING THE DOOR AND PUTTING HIS HEAD ROUND) It's me - Archie. Can I come in for a tick, Theo?
THEO Of course, of course. Come on in. Trouble, is it?
ARCHIE Oh, no - nothing like that - nothing like that at all. (ENTERS CARRYING TWO BOTTLES OF BEER, OPENED WITH THE GLASSES INVERTED ON THE NECKS) Just thought you might like a wet before you went on, as usual.
THEO Oh, right - ta. Won't say no.
ARCHIE Thought you wouldn't somehow. (CROSSES AND GIVES A BOTTLE AND GLASS TO THEODORE. Here are, then.
THEO Ta - sit yourself down. (TURNS ROUND) Throw the costumes off the armchair. Chuck 'em on the basket.
ARCHIE Oh, right - right. (REMOVES COSTUMES ETC)

4

THEO	That's seen better days, that has - that armchair. About time you got a new one for in here, I reckon. Eh, Archie?
ARCHIE	(LOOKING ROUND) Could do with a replacement or two in here, I agree. (SITS) Coo, that's better. Take the weight off the old plates of meat for a few ticks. First chance I've had tonight. I could put you in number two dressing room if you like. It's a bit bigger than this. But I know you'd rather be in this one - near to the stage and all that. You only have to say the word next time, you know.
THEO	No - this suits me fine - always been in here ever since I first played this theatre. Anyway, I know you like to drop in here for a chat and a beer and being right next to the stage, you can keep an ear cocked for what's going on. That's right, isn't it?
ARCHIE	Dead right, Theo my old lad - dead right.
THEO	(CONTINUING WITH HIS MAKE-UP) Been having a bit of an evening then, have you?
ARCHIE	In a sort of way, yes. I suppose you could say I have.
THEO	It wasn't Shirley again, was it?
ARCHIE	No - not this time - not Shirley. Quite her old self again, is our Shirl. She's queening it over the bar as usual just as though nothing had happened.
THEO	Good. I'm glad about that. Last thing I wanted to do was to upset her like that, believe me, Archie - the very last thing.
ARCHIE	Well, you did that all right. After your blood she was, last night. Make no mistake about that. After your blood with a vengeance, was our Shirley. I had the devil's own job stopping her from coming in here and scratching your eyes out at the very least.
THEO	Yes, well - as I said - I'm truly sorry. I thought everybody knew about Shirley's murky past. I never thought. I wouldn't have opened my mouth for the world if I'd have realised. I only just happened to mention it, in passing like, to Fred Bates round at 'The Grapes' and before you could say 'Bob's your uncle' it was all round the blooming theatre.
ARCHIE	I'll give you a bit of advice, Theo. Never tell anything to Fred if you want it kept secret - and that's a fact.
THEO	As I say, I didn't know it was a secret. I thought everyone knew she'd been inside.
ARCHIE	Oh, well, with a bit of luck, it'll all blow over in a day or two. All the same, I'd keep out of Shirley's way for bit if I was you.
THEO	Don't worry - I intend to. No point in looking for trouble, is there?
ARCHIE	No - no point at all.
THEO	What's up, then?
ARCHIE	It's Doris.
THEO	Doris? Oh, yes - what's up with her, then?
ARCHIE	(STAGE WHISPER) I shouldn't tell you, I suppose, but I know you won't tell anybody.
THEO	My name's not Fred Bates - don't worry.
ARCHIE	Exactly. All the same, don't say anything, will you?
THEO	Cross my heart and so on.
ARCHIE	Been to the doctor this afternoon. Just found out she's in the family way.
THEO	What - again? Silly kid!

ARCHIE	I agree. Bloody little fool! I don't know why she can't be more careful. You'd have thought she'd have learned her lesson after last time, wouldn't you?
THEO	That's a fact. How old is she?
ARCHIE	Doris? Oh, twenty-two or three - something like that.
THEO	You wouldn't believe it, would you? You'd think she'd have more sense.
ARCHIE	I don't see her mother looking after two kids - I don't really. I suppose I shall have to lose her this time. Pity - she's the best assistant stage manager I've ever had in this theatre. Real hot stuff is Doris.
THEO	So it seems.
ARCHIE	No, no - seriously - you know what I mean. Damn good little worker she is - works all hours that God sends. More or less runs the show, she does. Old George is O.K. on the get-ins and strikes and so on but he's getting past it, he really is - for a Stage Manager. I was thinking of pensioning him off soon but it looks as though I'll have to wait a bit now. God knows what I'm going to do. Have to think about it.
THEO	Upset, is she?
ARCHIE	I'll say. Floods of tears and so on. Took me ages to calm her down, it did.
THEO	Is she going to marry this one? Wedding bells, is it?
ARCHIE	I wouldn't be surprised if she did. Wouldn't surprise me at all. Dead serious she is about him - dead serious.
THEO	Well, what's she got to cry about then? Going to make an honest woman of her - what's she got to worry about?
ARCHIE	I don't think it's as straightforward as that somehow. She didn't say but I reckon there's something else troubling her. I tried to find out what it was but I couldn't get it out of her.
THEO	Perhaps he's not keen to do the right thing by her, as they say. Probably doesn't want to be saddled with the other kid.
ARCHIE	Could be - could be. You may be right.
THEO	Any idea who he is - the fellow I mean? Did she say?
ARCHIE	Oh, yes. She told me. Works down at Dean's, by all accounts - you know, the big store on the Parade.
THEO	Oh, yes?
ARCHIE	Only a bit of a kid, I believe - quite a few years younger than Doris but something of a lad, I gather. Quite a one for the ladies. I don't suppose our Doris is the only one by a long chalk. Perhaps she's found out he's been having it off with some other lass and so on.
THEO	You never know.
ARCHIE	Blimey - I wouldn't fancy being in his shoes if that's a fact, I wouldn't, I tell you. Temper! I've never known a girl who flies off the handle like she does. It's being Irish, I expect. Never lets it interfere with her work though, I'll say that for her. A real professional, is Doris, when she's backstage.
THEO	Oh, yes - she's a very good A.S.M. I've always thought that myself. Pity if you have to lose her.
ARCHIE	You can say that again.
THEO	This young lad - did she say what his name is?
ARCHIE	She did tell me but I can't remember rightly.
THEO	Works at Dean's, you say?

ARCHIE	That's right - some sort of window dresser or something, I think she said. Oh, that's right - I remember now - name of Charlie something or the other.
THEO	Charlie Pride, was it?
ARCHIE	I think it was - yes, Charlie Pride. I remember thinking to myself - Pride comes before a fall. (LAUGHS) See what I mean?
THEO	You've been watching too many of us comics, Archie my boy. That's your trouble. We'll have to put you on the stage one of these days - just see if we don't.
ARCHIE	Not if I know anything about it, you won't - oh, no - not on your blooming life. This Charlie Pride - do you know him, then?
THEO	Oh, yes - I know Charlie all right.
ARCHIE	Well now - there's a coincidence. Nice lad, is he?
THEO	You could say that - yes.
ARCHIE	Oh, that's good - good. Perhaps it'll all turn out all right in the end after all. (AFTER A PAUSE) Fancy another beer? It won't take a tick.
THEO	It's all right, Archie my old love, thank you. This'll do me fine. I musn't get pissed before I go on, must I? You never know - I might wet my knickers.
ARCHIE	Oh, right.
THEO	This boy friend of Doris's. Is she sure he was the father?
ARCHIE	Swears blind he is. Why?
THEO	Nothing - nothing. Just wondered, that's all. Must be quite a lad, young Charlie - quite a lad. (AFTER A PAUSE) What's the house like tonight?
ARCHIE	Bit thin - bit thin. Be like this now till the panto, I expect.
THEO	Bound to be.
ARCHIE	You fixed up this year?
THEO	Three weeks up in Stirling. Start rehearsals next week.
ARCHIE	Stirling, eh? You want to watch it, you do. All those Scotsmen in their kilts.
THEO	(NOT OFFENDED) Just you watch it, Archie Briggs. Just because you're an old mate of mine you think you can say anything and get away with it, don't you?
ARCHIE	Who are you trying to kid? I know you, Theo. Should do after all these years.
THEO	If you don't by now you never will.
ARCHIE	I'll say this much for you - never try to pretend you're not like that though, do you?
THEO	Watch it, mate. You'll have me run in one of these days if you're not careful.
ARCHIE	I'll watch it - don't you worry.
THEO	Anyway, I'm getting past it now, Archie - getting past it.
ARCHIE	I'll believe that when I see it, I will. Reckon the only time you'll be past it is when they screw you down in your box.
THEO	Maybe, maybe. That'll not be for some time yet, I hope. Good for a few more years going round the halls, I reckon.
ARCHIE	Don't you sometimes get browned off with living out of a suitcase - stopping in a different town each week?
THEO	Can't say I do, Archie, to tell you the truth. It's my life, isn't it? I wouldn't want to change it for anything different. I've got no roots anywhere - no real responsibilities. I've got a lot of good friends like you all over the country.

	It's nice to see them from time to time. Never stay too long in one place. Might wear out my welcome, if you see what I mean.
ARCHIE	Yes. Played this theatre a good few times over the years, haven't you?
THEO	At least twice a year for ... must be getting on for twenty years, I suppose.
ARCHIE	Ever thought of trying to get on television? It's getting very popular.
THEO	Not interested, Archie - not interested. Once give 'em your act on television and they've all seen it. See what I mean?
ARCHIE	There is that, of course. I hadn't thought about it like that. But it's catching on, you know - no doubt at all about that. Audiences in the theatres aren't what they used to be at one time. Rather stay at home and watch a little box than make the effort to come out at night.
THEO	Oh, well - if the worst comes to the worst, I could always put away my bra and buy a pub or something.
ARCHIE	What - down at the docks, eh? With all those randy sailors.
THEO	I'm not warning you again, Archie Briggs. Anyway, as I said, I'm getting past it. I'm beginning to feel my age.
ARCHIE	As long as that's all you're feeling. (LAUGHS HEARTILY)
THEO	At it again, are you? Trying to take the bread out of my mouth?
ARCHIE	I've told you - I'm not interested in treading the boards. Mind you, I reckon I could do as well as some of 'em.
THEO	Better than a lot, I wouuldn't wonder. I don't know where they get some of 'em from, I don't really.
ARCHIE	I won't book 'em, you know - a lot of 'em. I've no time for a lot of these new acts. Still wet behind the ears, some of 'em.
THEO	Yes, you book good acts here, Archie. I'll say that for you. One or two of 'em are getting a bit long in the tooth but, by and large, good acts.
ARCHIE	I try, Theo, I try. But it isn't always easy to find the good ones.
THEO	Talking of getting long in the tooth, isn't it about time Carlos and Queenie thought of packing it in?
ARCHIE	Oh, I don't know. They're not too bad.
THEO	They almost gave her the bird on Wednesday, I hear.
ARCHIE	Just one or two drunks, that's all.
THEO	Stupid old cow! I don't know why she didn't chuck it in years ago. What a bloody life, eh? Standing there in her sequined knickers every night with Carlos shooting clay pipes out of her mouth!
ARCHIE	You've really got it in for Queenie, haven't you?
THEO	Can't stand the woman - but it's not just that. Look, Archie, I think there's something you ought to know. I've been trying to make my mind up all the week whether or not to tell you but now I think it'd be better if I did. Only fair to all concerned.
ARCHIE	(RISING) Go on then. Serious, is it? (MOVING TO THEO'S LEFT)
THEO	I was on the same bill with them at Huddersfield last week.
ARCHIE	Yes?
THEO	I go on before them here but, last week, I followed them.

I got down early one night - Tuesday I think it was - yes, Tuesday. They called me too early so I stood in the wings and took in part of their act. Carlos. was drunk, I swear he was. I don't mean just a bit tipsy. I mean real bloody drunk. His hands were shaking like a jelly. I could see from where I was standing on the side. Fortunately nothing went wrong - he got through the act all right but it was a bloody miracle, I can tell you.

ARCHIE   Oh, I wouldn't worry. Always been a bit too fond of the bottle, has Carlos, but it never seems to effect his act.

THEO   Not up till now, maybe, but this was different. I've never seen him like that before - never. If he goes on like that, one of these nights he's going to miss and our Queenie will be sporting her sequined knickers up there with the angels. Don't say I didn't warn you.

ARCHIE   You think it's that serious, do you?

THEO   I'm sure it is. Anyway, that's not all by a long chalk. The following night, he went off after his act and left his loaded pistol lying about in the wings.

ARCHIE   The bloody fool! That couldn't happen here anyway. I have very strict rules about firearms in this theatre. I have to. The Watch Committee is red hot in this town. They'd have my guts for garters if that happened in this theatre. As soon as the artist comes into the theatre, they hand over their firearms and straight into the theatre safe they go. The Stage Manager and the A.S.M. are the only ones, apart from the Bar Manageress and me who have keys to the safe. The artist get their firearms handed to them just before the act - after they've been called. Then, after the act, back into the safe they go until the artist leaves the theatre. What they do with them then is up to them. It's not my responsibility then.

THEO   Very wise that is, Archie, very wise. All the same, I'm dead worried about Carlos. Look, I'll tell you how worried I am. I had a quiet word with the manager there - you know - Bert Carter. Took it very serious, did Bert - very serious indeed. He told me he wasn't going to book them for his theatre again - not after what had happened. Too much of a risk, he reckons. He had a word with Carlos. I don't know what he told him but I reckon it's curtains for Carlos and Queenie at the Empire, Huddersfield.

ARCHIE   Good manager - Bert. Known him for years. If he gave 'em their marching orders I reckon he must have thought there was good reason all right. I'll have to think about this - have to think about it very seriously. (TO CENTRE STAGE) Thanks for the tip, Theo.

THEO   Well, I thought I ought to mention it. Only fair to all concerned. By the way, you won't tell 'em I told you, will you?

ARCHIE   Course not - wouldn't dream of it. You know me, Theo - soul of discretion, I am. I'll just say I heard it on the grape-vine like.

THEO   I'd be obliged, Archie.

ARCHIE   (TURNING TO THEO) She fancies you, you know - always has.

THEO   Well, the feeling's not mutual, I assure you. She makes me

9

	sick, she does - mincing about displaying her fat arse to all and sundry. It isn't as though she's got any sort of figure.
ARCHIE	I've seen worse in my time.
THEO	Maybe. All the same, you'd have thought she'd have got the message by now, wouldn't you? I wouldn't even to bother to look up if Marilyn Monroe walked in here stark naked. She must realise that.
ARCHIE	I think I'll go and get myself another beer. Quite sure you don't want another?
THEO	Positive, Archie. Thanks all the same. How long have I got?
ARCHIE	(LOOKING AT HIS WATCH) Ages yet - a good quarter.
THEO	(WHO, BY NOW, HAS FINISHED HIS MAKE-UP) I like to get in nice and early. Like to give myself plenty of time - hate rushing things. Need lots of time these days anyway - takes a lot of covering up - the old phizog.
ARCHIE	Real artist, you are, Theo. Perfectionist, aren't you? Everything's got to be spot on, hasn't it?
THEO	Of course. Tonight's audience have paid their hard-earned money to see me and the others. They deserve the best we can give 'em. That's what I believe, anyway.
ARCHIE	Wish they all thought your way, Theo. Some of these kids - they're not real pros, you know. Well - mustn't stand here chewing the rag. Must go and get a drink and see how things are going. (GOES TO DOOR AND OPENS IT - SOUND OF APPLAUSE) That'll be Peppie and His Dogs just finishing. There's Andy Penfold and Mick to go on before you. Well, I'll be back in a tick unless I get waylaid by Queenie or something. (STARTS TO GO OUT) Talk of the devil!
THEO	It's not her, is it?
ARCHIE	'Fraid so, old man. Bearing down on this door she is like the Queen Mary coming into port!
THEO	Tell her I'm not here. Tell her I've got the plague. Tell her any bloody thing but keep her out of here for God's sake!
ARCHIE	(WHISPERING) Too late! She's just about to make an entrance. Hard luck old man. See you later. Don't do anything that I wouldn't do and if you can't be good be careful.
THEO	(THROWING A SHOE) Get out!

ARCHIE EXITS AND LEAVES THE DOOR OPEN FOR QUEENIE WHO ENTERS AT ONCE. SHE IS WEARING A BRIGHT COLOURED WRAP OVER HER STAGE COSTUME. SHE IS LATE MIDDLE-AGED AND PLUMPISH. HER HAIR IS DYED PLATINUM BLONDE.

QUEENIE	Can I come in, love? (DOESN'T WAIT FOR AN ANSWER)
THEO	It looks as though you're in, doesn't it?
QUEENIE	(BENDING DOWN) Someone's dropped their shoe. (MOVES TO LEFT OF THEO) Is it yours, love?
THEO	Get lost!
QUEENIE	(FLUTTERING HER FALSE EYELASHES) Who isn't in a very good mood today, eh? Get out of bed the wrong side this morning, did we? Or did some lucky lady push you out, eh?
THEO	Did you hear me telling you to get out? I'm just going to get into my costume.
QUEENIE	Temper! Temper! That's no way to speak to the light of your life, is it?
THEO	I'm no light in your life and you bloody know it.

QUEENIE	More's the pity. (MOVING TO HIM) I could be good for you, you know.
THEO	(TURNING TO HER) Look, Queenie, I'm not bloody interested. How many more times have I got to tell you?
QUEENIE	Come off it, love. I know you don't mean that. Just playing hard to get, aren't you?
THEO	Will you please go back to your own dressing room and leave me in peace to get my costume on? I'm on shortly. I don't like to be hurried.
QUEENIE	I'll just go and sit over there in that chair and ...
THEO	(RISING AND GRABBING HER) Look, Queenie, I've asked you nicely and you've taken no notice so I'm going to have to lay it on the line. I don't fancy you. I never have fancied you and I think you're just a fat old bag and I wouldn't touch you with a barge pole. Get it?
QUEENIE	Don't you talk to me like that.
THEO	I'll talk to you any way I please.
QUEENIE	I know all about you, I do.
THEO	Oh, yes? What do you know?
QUEENIE	You're nothing but a bloody fairy - that's what you are - a bloody old fairy. I've heard things about you, I have.
THEO	What have you heard?
QUEENIE	Oh, yes - you'd like to know, wouldn't you?
THEO	Tell me, you old cow, what have you heard? (TWISTS HER ARM) What have you heard?
QUEENIE	Leave go my arm. I'll fetch Carlos to you - you see if I don't.
THEO	What - that drunken old has-been? Don't make me laugh.
QUEENIE	Don't you say things like that about my Carlos. He's worth ten of the like of you, he is. At least he doesn't muck about with eighteen year old lads, he doesn't.
THEO	What are you on about, eh? Go on - tell me.
QUEENIE	That's got you worried, hasn't it, eh? You didn't know that I knew that, did you? But I do, see. I know all about you and young Charlie - him that works at Dean's. I've heard from a woman I know who works there on a Saturday. Bloody disgusting I call it. You ought to be ashamed of yourself, you had - a man of your age leading young lads astray. Young enough to be your son, he is. Got a girl friend, he had - going steady, they were, until you started your dirty ...
THEO	Shut up! Shut up, do you hear?
QUEENIE	They lock people up for what you've done - do you know that, eh? Put 'em in prison where they belong - where they can't interfere with young lads. Prison's too good for 'em, that's what I say. Your sort need castrating, that's what I say.
THEO	Shut up, you foul-mouthed old bitch.
QUEENIE	Fairies like you make me want to throw up.
THEO	Get out of here! Get out before I send for the manager and have you thrown out.
QUEENIE	Who? Your bloody mate, Archie Briggs? I'd like to see him try, that's all. God knows what he sees in you. I'm sure I don't. Always in and out of here, he is. What is it? Is he a bloody fairy as well?
THEO	(SLAPPING HER FACE) Right - you asked for that. Now, shut your stupid trap and get out of my dressing room.

11

QUEENIE	(NURSING HER FACE) You bastard! Gone too far this time, you have. I'll have the police to you, I will. (TO DOOR) I'm not joking, you know - I mean it. I'm going to the police and I'm going to tell 'em all about you. You just see if I don't. You don't lay your dirty hands on me and get away with it, you don't. (EXIT)
THEO	Stupid old bag!

HE GOES TO THE DRESSING TABLE AND PICKS UP HIS COSTUME AND PUTS IT ON. HE REMOVES HIS TROUSERS AND PUTS ON A PAIR OF LONG OLD-FASHIONED DRAWERS. THEN HE PUTS ON A HEAVILY PADDED BRA AND FINALLY THE DRESS. THE DOOR OPENS AND ARCHIE COMES IN WITH A BOTTLE OF BEER.

THEO	Just in time, Archie. Zip me up, will you?
ARCHIE	(MOVING TO THEO AND ZIPPING UP THE BACK OF THE DRESS) What's up with our Queenie, then? Just passed her in the corridor - face like thunder, she'd got. You've given her the brush-off then? (TO CENTRE STAGE)
THEO	(PICKING UP HIS WIG AND SITTING AT THE DRESSING TABLE TO PUT IT ON) You could say that - yes.
ARCHIE	Proper upset, she looked.
THEO	I hit her.
ARCHIE	(TURNING TO THEO) You did what?
THEO	I slapped her across the face. She asked for it - the foul-mouthed old bitch.
ARCHIE	Maybe she did but I don't think you should have hit her, all the same.
THEO	You didn't hear what she said.
ARCHIE	No - but you shouldn't have hit her, should you? It's not like you to do a thing like that, Theo. What was it she said?
THEO	Forget it. It doesn't matter.
ARCHIE	It must have been pretty serious for you to have belted her, I reckon.
THEO	Accused me of leading young lads astray - that's what.
ARCHIE	I see.
THEO	Do you - see, I mean?
ARCHIE	Grain of truth in it, was there?
THEO	I swear to you, Archie that I've never led young lads astray, as she puts it. I admit I ... how shall I put it? Well, I strike up relationships with young men but they're old enough to know what it's all about. But young lads - never in my life.
ARCHIE	Look, Theo - I don't want to know - that's your business. I don't want to pry into your private life. I've known you for a good many years, haven't I? We've been good friends - at least I like to think we have. I always enjoy it when you play this theatre - enjoy our little chats. I've never asked you any questions, have I? Oh, I've ribbed you from time to time but there was no harm meant, I assure you. What you do outside this theatre doesn't concern me. As long as you do your act and the audiences still want to pay to come and see you perform, I'll go on booking you two or three times a year. But try not to bring your private life into this theatre. That's all I ask. If you do, I'll be compelled to do something about it. Otherwise - I'm like the three wise monkies. Get it?
THEO	O.K. Archie - that's fair enough. Let's leave it at that, eh?

ARCHIE	Suits me.
THEO	I'm sorry if hitting Queenie caused any sort of trouble for you. She just got up my wick and I clouted her, that's all.
ARCHIE	Right, Theo - forget it then. I'll just go and have a word - smooth things over a bit if I can. They go on after you. I don't want any more trouble tonight.
THEO	O.K. See you later.
ARCHIE	Right. Shan't be a tick. (EXIT)

THEO CONTINUES TO MAKE ADJUSTMENTS TO HIS WIG, PUTS ON SOME SHOES AND THEN CARRIES OUT SOME SLIGHT ALTERATIONS TO HIS MAKE-UP. THE DOOR BURSTS OPEN AND DORIS MALONE RUSHES IN. SHE IS IN A BLAZING TEMPER.

DORIS	You bastard! You dirty, rotten bastard!
THEO	(RISING AND TURNING TO HER) What's the matter with you? What the hell's going on around here?
DORIS	Queenie's just told me.
THEO	Told you what?
DORIS	About you and Charlie.
THEO	Stupid bitch! What did she tell you?
DORIS	You know damn well what she told me. Told me that you'd been messing about with my Charlie. That's what she told me.
THEO	She wants to mind her own business, does Queenie. It's not got anything to do with her - nothing at all.
DORIS	It's to do with me though, hasn't it? I love Charlie - do you know that? I was going to marry the lad, did you know that?
THEO	I have heard - yes, but only tonight. I didn't know before tonight, I swear. I didn't even know you were going out with him. He didn't say a word about you.
DORIS	No. Well, he wasn't likely to, was he?
THEO	(MOVING TO HER) Look, Doris - I'm sorry. I truly am. I had no idea he was anything to do with you. I wouldn't do anything to hurt you, you must know that.
DORIS	But you have, haven't you? (TO CENTRE STAGE) I still don't really believe it - I just don't. He's just been on the phone to me and do you know what? I'm going to have his kid and I've just told him - he didn't know before. He said he was thrilled and he said he'd start making arrangements for the wedding. And all the time, he'd been messing about with you. I just can't believe it. (DROPS INTO ARMCHAIR) I didn't know he was like that - I didn't really. Oh, God, what am I going to do? (STARTS TO CRY)
THEO	(MOVING TO THE SIDE OF THE ARMCHAIR AND THEN CROUCHING DOWN) Doris love, listen to me - please. Believe me, I'm sorry. I'm desperately sorry. I didn't know. I really didn't. If there is anything I can do to try to put things right between you and Charlie ...
DORIS	He's a darling fellow - he really is. I know he's younger than me but I didn't think that mattered. He knows all about me - about young Mike, I mean. He said he didn't mind. He said he was prepared to marry me and take on young Mike as well. And just now, when I told him about the baby, he was thrilled - he really was. (LOOKING UP) You won't tell anybody about this, will you?
THEO	No, Doris - I won't. I give you my solemn promise.

13

DORIS	I thought everything was going to be fine from now on and then Queenie comes and whispers to me about you and Charlie and my whole world falls apart.
THEO	Look, Doris - I won't see him again. I won't really. I'm sure that everything will turn out all right. I wouldn't have had this happen for the world if I'd known. I've always been fond of you, you know that, Doris (PUTS HIS ARM AROUND HER)
DORIS	And a damn fine way you had of showing it, hadn't you?
THEO	Oh, Doris.
DORIS	And take your blasted hands off me. Don't think you get round me.
THEO	(REMOVING HIS ARM AND RISING - TURNING AWAY) I don't know what more to say. I've said I'm sorry. (HE IS QUIETLY CRYING)
DORIS	(RISING) God, you're pathetic. You think that all you've got to say is that you're sorry and it's all over - forgotten as though it had never been. Is that what you think, eh? Well, you've got another damn think coming, Theo Mason. You haven't heard the last of this. (MOVING TO HIM) I'll get you for this. I'll get you for this even if it earns me a place in hell's fire.
THEO	Doris - please.
DORIS	I've got to get back. The act's nearly finished. (QUICK EXIT)

THEO STANDS AND STARES AFTER HER IN SILENCE AND THEN SLOWLY GOES TO THE DRESSING TABLE, PICKS UP SOME LONG BLACK GLOVES AND STARTS TO PUT THEM ON. ARCHIE ENTERS

ARCHIE	Was that Doris I saw coming out of here?
THEO	Yes.
ARCHIE	What did she want?
THEO	I .. I .. only to tell me I was on in two minutes.
ARCHIE	I see. Theo ... I've just done a bloody stupid thing.
THEO	Join the club. Why, what's happened?
ARCHIE	It's Carlos and Queenie. When I went to see them just now, I suddenly took the bull by the horns and told them I wouldn't be booking them into this theatre again. And then I went and said that, as far as I was concerned, they were finished.
THEO	Oh, no!
ARCHIE	I only intended to go in and talk to Queenie to calm her before she went on but then she started hurling abuse at me. Threatened me, she did. Said that if ever I booked you into this theatre again, she'd go to the police and tell them something or the other about you. She didn't say what. Then I just saw red and let 'em have the lot. I should have waited until the end of the week, I know that, but the harm's done now. All hell let loose. Carlos is carrying on like a raving maniac.
THEO	You didn't tell them you wouldn't book them again because of what happened in Huddersfield last week, did you?
ARCHIE	Well - yes I did. I know I shouldn't have.
THEO	But they'll know it was me who told you. I was the only one on the bill with them at Huddersfield who's playing here this week.
ARCHIE	I didn't say you told me.

14

THEO	You didn't have to - they're not that thick. They'll put two and two together and ... (SOUND OF APPLAUSE) God - that's me. I'm on. (RUSHES TO DOOR)
ARCHIE	Good luck, mate. Slay 'em, eh?
THEO	Just so long as somebody doesn't slay me first. (EXIT)

ARCHIE GOES UP TO THE DOOR AND CLOSES IT. HE THEN TURNS ON THE TANNOY WHICH IS BY THE DOOR AND THEN COLLECTS HIS BEER FROM THE END OF THE DRESSING TABLE WHERE HE LEFT IT ON HIS LAST EXIT. HE CROSSES TO THE ARMCHAIR, SITS AND POURS HIS BEER. THE INTRO TO THEO'S ACT IS HEARD FROM THE TANNOY. THIS IS FOLLOWED BY HIS ACT EXACTLY AS AT THE BEGINNING OF THE PLAY AND WITH AUDIENCE LAUGHTER. ARCHIE SETTLES BACK AND LISTENS TO THE BEGINNING OF THE ACT AND LAUGHS FROM TIME TO TIME. SUDDENLY, THE DOOR OPENS AND DORIS RUSHES IN.

DORIS	I thought I'd find you here. (TURNS DOWN THE TANNOY TO HALF VOLUME)
ARCHIE	What's up?. Not more trouble, is it? One more night like this and I'll give up.
DORIS	It's about Carlos and Queenie.
ARCHIE	Yes, Doris - I know. It's my fault. I said something to them to upset them. I'll just finish my beer and then I'll go and have another word with them - see if I can calm them down a bit before they go on. (LOOKS AT HIS WATCH) There's a few minutes yet. Theo's got almost another fifteen.
DORIS	You don't understand. Carlos is not in his dressing room.
ARCHIE	(RISING AND PUTTING THE BEER ON THE HAMPER) Where is he then?
DORIS	In the wings. I don't like it. He's just been to me to issue his gun. I told him he'd have to wait. till he went on but he got nasty and said he'd got to have it now. He said he needed to make an adjustment to the safety catch or something. He was very persistent.|
ARCHIE	You didn't give it to him, did you?
DORIS	I didn't see how I could refuse him. He said he had to make this repair and unless I gave him the gun, he wouldn't be able to do his act.
ARCHIE	So you did give it to him?
DORIS	I had to. All the same, I wish now that I hadn't. I got it out of the safe and he just snatched it from me and rushed off into the wings. I don't like it. I don't like it at all. Will you come and have a word with Carlos - see if you can get him to go back into his dressing room? I asked him not to stand in the wings but he just swore at me and wouldn't shift. He's in a terrible state.
ARCHIE	Where's George? Can't he get him out of the wings?
DORIS	He's up in the flies. The cloth on number two bar's stuck and he's gone up to try to fix it. Do please come, Mr Briggs. I'm scared stiff something terrible is going to happen.
ARCHIE	Right. I'll come straight way. Where's Queenie?
DORIS	She was still in her dressing room when I came to find you but I don't know if she's there now.
ARCHIE	Right - come along then. (MOVING TO THE DOOR) You go and look for Queenie. If she's still in her dressing room, keep her there and I'll go and get Carlos out of the wings.

DORIS	Right.
ARCHIE	George is probably down from the flies by now. I'll get him to give me a hand with Carlos. We'll drag him out if we have to. God, what a night!

THERE IS THE SOUND OF A SHOT

DORIS	Oh, Jesus and Mary! (STARTS TO SCREAM)
ARCHIE	Come on, Doris pull yourself together. We've got to go and find out what's happened. Doris - this is not like you. Come on, control yourself.

QUEENIE RUSHES IN

QUEENIE	Quick! Quick! Come quick, for God's sake!
ARCHIE	What is it? What's happened?
QUEENIE	I think he's dead.
ARCHIE	Who's dead? Who is it?
QUEENIE	It's Carlos He's shot himself.

DORIS STARTS TO SCREAM AGAIN AS ARCHIE RUSHES OUT

BLACKOUT

NOTE

THE TIMING OF THEO'S ACT AT THE BEGINNING OF THE PLAY IS SUCH THAT WHEN IT IS RE-PLAYED THROUGH THE TANNOY DURING THE LAST SCENE, THE ENDING SHOULD COME EXACTLY ON CUE. HOWEVER, THIS CAN BE ADJUSTED BY SHORTENING OR LENGTHENING THE TIME THAT ARCHIE LISTENS TO THE ACT BEFORE DORIS'S ENTRANCE.